*Kristi M. Lee*

# The Ocean Springs Book

by

## Kristin M. Lee

with illustrations by Oliver Preus

**Special thanks to:**
My friends and family for the encouragement, love, and support
I needed to meet this huge goal of mine.

Ocean Springs Chamber of Commerce, city employees, business owners,
teachers, residents, and visitors that have made
Ocean Springs a desirable place for my family to reside.

**Acknowledgments:**
Oliver for turning my ideas into reality through his incredible artwork and book design.
"I can't thank you enough for all of your hard work in making this book possible!"

Jamie B. for her much appreciated editing skills.

Steve for working with us through the unfamiliar printing process.

---

There are many other deserving locations & events that make Ocean Springs
such a great place to live & visit. And, as hard as I tried,
I was unable to fit all of the goodness of OS into this book.
I am sorry.

---

The Ocean Springs Book, by Kristin Lee; illustrated by Oliver Preus . - 1st ed.
Copyright © 2018 by Kristin Lee
No part of this book may be used or reproduced in any form without written permission
from the author.
All rights reserved. Published by Egg & Vine Publishing Co.
Printed in USA by FCI Digital
978-1-61850-157-8

For our families, friends, and ALL who share a love for Ocean Springs

Although the entire Mississippi Gulf Coast may be beautiful and fun, if you haven't been to Ocean Springs, your trip is hardly done!

It is a town you just don't want to miss,
Where livin' is easy and visiting is bliss.

You can play in the parks, or at the beach in the sun.

You can can see some fine art. Why, you've just begun!

If you want to check out local theater, music and art, the Mary C. is a GREAT place to start!

Explore the unique works of the Anderson family by visiting Realizations, The Walter Anderson Museum of Art or stopping by Shearwater Pottery.

People are running, biking and nightlife lovin'.

Miner's Doll and Toy Store or Sugar and Spice are places kids go to find something nice.

Hillyer House and Lee Tracy are a couple more stores you may want to see.

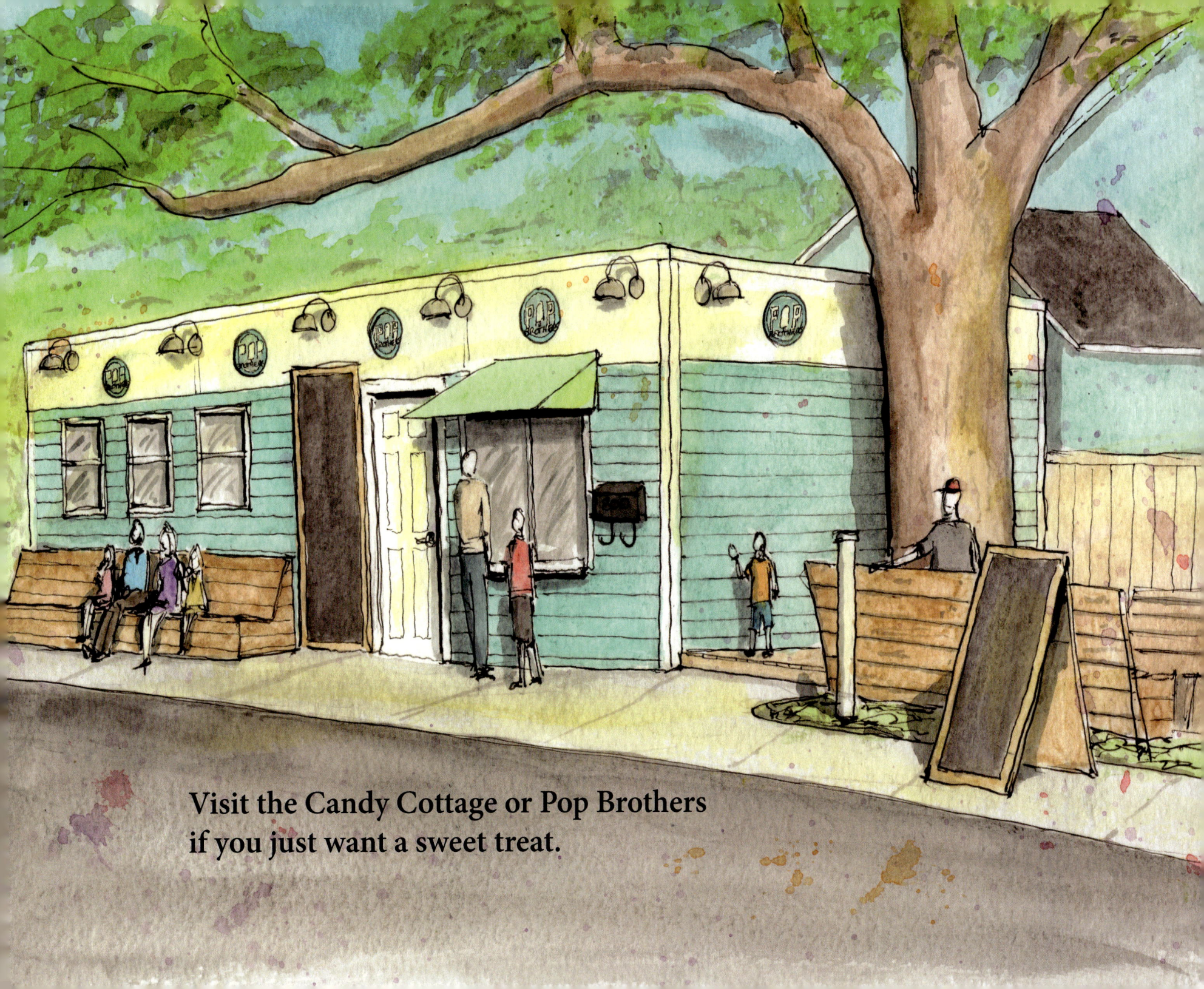

Visit the Candy Cottage or Pop Brothers
if you just want a sweet treat.

You can also enjoy the soda fountain at Lovelace, just down the street.

Savor a hot cup of coffee at The Greenhouse on Porter, with the most delicious biscuits you'll definitely want to order!

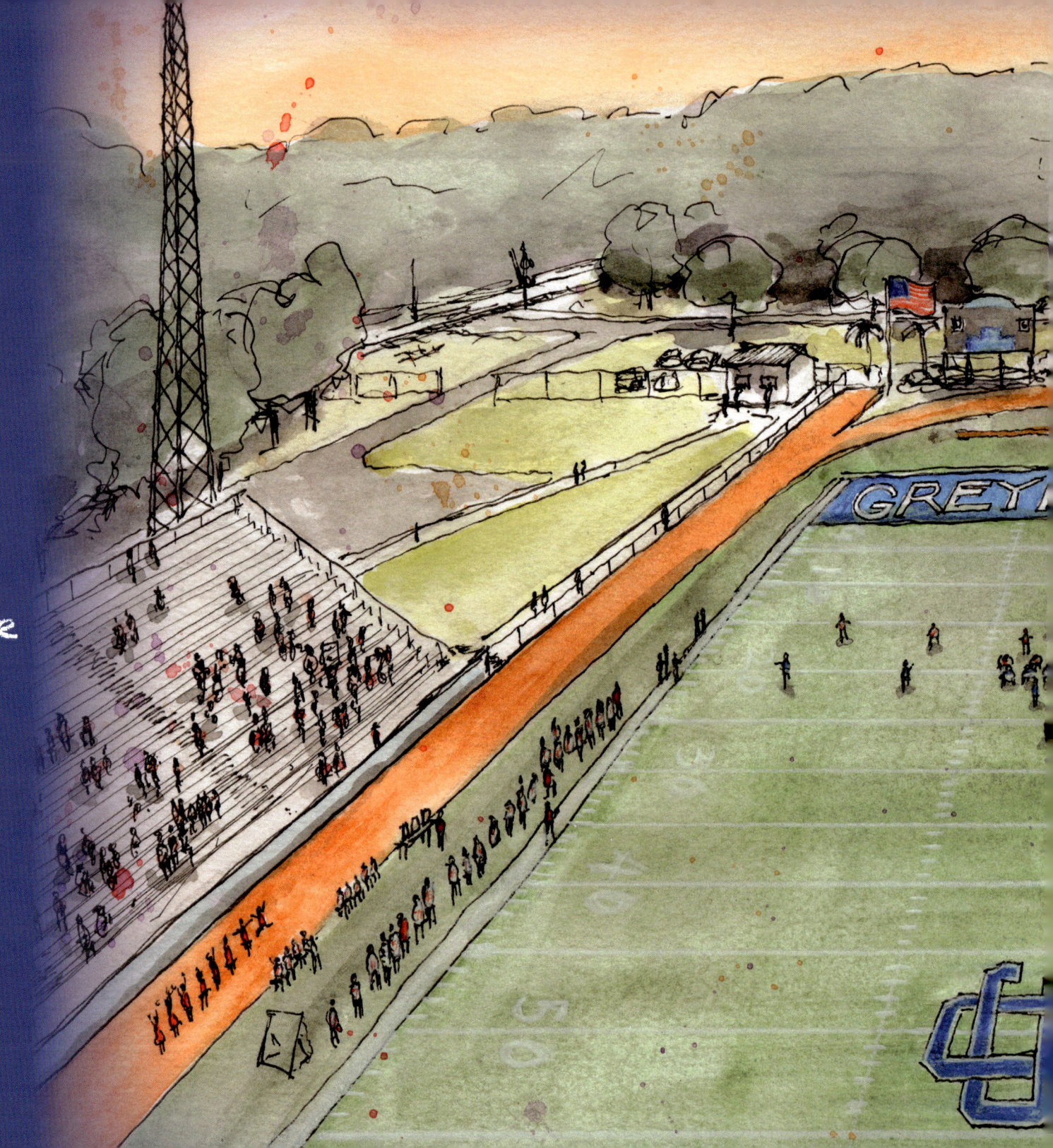

Under the Friday night lights, the stands are filled with blue and grey.

We sing our national anthem and bow our heads to pray.

There's the Gulf Islands National Seashore Park that we enjoy so much! It's the place to learn about local wildlife you can see and touch.

On Sundays, we attend churches like First Baptist, St. Al's and First Pres, just to name a few. We love to worship and would be happy to have you!

There are fresh markets on Saturdays, fishing and regattas too.
Shopping and touring historical homes are some more things you can do.

The Peter Anderson Arts and Crafts Festival and Cruisin' The Coast are the two biggest events that bring others most. They're great for seeing old friends and greeting those visiting the coast.

You can rest your head at The Roost or The Inn.

What a fun way for your day to begin (or end)!